Ellen Rose Galvão Helal
Thelma Helena Costa Chahini

Teaching qualifications in the context of inclusion

Ellen Rose Galvão Helal
Thelma Helena Costa Chahini

Teaching qualifications in the context of inclusion

ScienciaScripts

Imprint
Any brand names and product names mentioned in this book are subject to trademark, brand or patent protection and are trademarks or registered trademarks of their respective holders. The use of brand names, product names, common names, trade names, product descriptions etc. even without a particular marking in this work is in no way to be construed to mean that such names may be regarded as unrestricted in respect of trademark and brand protection legislation and could thus be used by anyone.

Cover image: www.ingimage.com

This book is a translation from the original published under ISBN 978-613-9-64121-5.

Publisher:
Sciencia Scripts
is a trademark of
Dodo Books Indian Ocean Ltd. and OmniScriptum S.R.L publishing group

120 High Road, East Finchley, London, N2 9ED, United Kingdom
Str. Armeneasca 28/1, office 1, Chisinau MD-2012, Republic of Moldova, Europe
Printed at: see last page
ISBN: 978-620-7-72832-9

PRESENTATION

This book, "Teacher Qualification in the Context of Inclusion", is the result of further studies and reflections on the teaching-learning process of children with special educational needs, as well as the social attitudes found in educational institutions.

A critical-reflexive approach is taken to the process of inclusion in early childhood education institutions, as well as the initial and continuing training of primary school teachers within the principles of Inclusive Education.

It should be emphasised that teacher qualification is a fundamental condition in the context of inclusion, since the target audience of special education needs specialised educational care, not only in multifunctional resource rooms, but also in regular classrooms.

We wish you good reading and many reflections.

The authors

SUMMARY

CHAPTER 1

INTRODUCTION

Given the purpose of Early Childhood Education and as an integral part of Basic Education, as set out in Law No. 9394/96, it can be inferred that integration is something inherent to the human being, and so, in the face of the educational process, it must be taken into account that the child's development is associated with affective, cognitive, physical and social aspects.

It should be pointed out that working with Special Education in the context of Basic Education, but precisely at the Early Childhood Education stage, requires new perspectives on pedagogical practice, as there is an urgent need to transpose the purely technical dimension into a more dynamic practice that respects the specificities of the students, understanding them as beings who must have their differences respected, as well as learning to be and live with themselves, their colleagues and the environment in an articulated and gradual way.

The interest in this study arose because of the various particularities that have entered classrooms and, with them, the difficulty of integrating and working with special children. In contact with a student with special needs, this led me to reflect that, in fact, there was no knowledge, no support from the public institution and no favourable means to develop the proper work with that child.

Faced with these circumstances, and although in theory they were complying with the law, it is known that the physically disabled and those with special needs have had their educational policies revised and public policies created through movements and struggles by the less favoured classes so that they could be attended to in a more equal way, although it is also known that this falls far short of what is actually expected.

Just as prominently, the training of education professionals should include curricular matrices that really help to ensure that education for special needs is effective, especially for early childhood education professionals.

Given this context, the question arises: what are the perceptions of pedagogues working in Early Childhood Education in relation to their professional qualifications for the care of children considered to be the target audience of Special Education?

It is hypothesised that, based on the curriculum matrix of the Pedagogy courses offered by Higher Education Institutions in São Luís, they are insufficient for the Pedagogue to be able to instruct a child with special needs in regular classrooms.

In order to respond to the problem, the general objective was to investigate the perceptions of pedagogues who work in early childhood education in relation to their professional qualifications to care for children considered to be the target audience of special education. The specific objectives were: to recognise whether the contents and internships of the Pedagogy course contribute to working with children with disabilities, global developmental disorders and high abilities; to find out what knowledge the participants have in relation to the care of children with disabilities, global developmental disorders and high abilities; to recognise whether the Pedagogue training policies include working with children with disabilities, global developmental disorders and high abilities.

This study is divided into six chapters, the first of which contains an introduction setting out the reasons and objectives for the research.

Chapter two presents the framework of laws that guide both Early Childhood Education and Special Education throughout the child's educational process. Its sub-chapters discuss terminology in learning and also in Early Childhood Education, with a view to demonstrating the range of "different" people in the classroom. It also deals with the process of including young children with disabilities, global development disorders and high abilities.

Chapter three shows how the process of setting up the Pedagogy course has taken place over the years. Amid reports, opinions, resolutions and laws, the qualification of the pedagogue from the perspective of inclusion is still lacking in terms of actually meeting the specific needs of children with disabilities.

The fourth chapter presents the methodology used to carry out this research, which is exploratory and descriptive in nature, with a bibliographical and documentary survey. Its sub-chapters present the location, emphasising that it was not chosen specifically due to the lack of consent from managers at both the public and private institutions. As for the participants, eleven teachers contributed to this research. The data collection instrument used was a semi-structured interview applied using a script containing seven questions. To collect the data, the interviews were duly recorded and later transcribed so that the results could be tabulated and analysed.

Chapter five presents the results, analysis and discussion collected, where we observed a significant gap in pedagogical training when it comes to Special Education, as well as the importance for professional pedagogues to seek training to subsidise possibilities for working with the target audience of Special Education.

This work concludes in chapter six with final considerations, emphasising that the subject in question will always deserve attention and greater depth given the importance of offering an equal education to any and all school-age citizens, especially those in early childhood education.

CHAPTER 2

EARLY CHILDHOOD EDUCATION AND SPECIAL EDUCATION

The mother's womb is a child's first world of contact. There is literally a bond that allows not only the exchange of fluids, but above all, of emotions. There, communication is possible from the moment the parents and other family members talk to the baby, dosing the tone of voice and touch, and in this interaction there is an exchange of belonging.

With the same care, a child's first contact with school must be carefully considered, as it goes hand in hand with their cognitive development and skills, as well as their emotional development, which is much sharper and more intense in childhood.

With this in mind, as well as taking care of the physical space, it is just as important to select the people who will be dealing with this child, emphasising that this phase is the most important of all in the entire educational process. Although this should be the case, education for young children, legally known as Early Childhood Education, has gone through a long historical process to become established and recognised, in which, initially, these aspects were not really taken into account.

The reasons for thinking about Early Childhood Education were marked by the birth of capitalism and urbanisation, which led to an imminent need for women to enter the labour market, as well as the reorganisation and new structure of the family, in the sense that women sometimes became the mainstay of family support, which led to the need for a suitable place for children to stay, considering their needs in terms of care, which are paramount and, according to Sanches (2003, p. 63)

> In Brazil, crèches emerged at the end of the 19th century as a result of the country's industrialisation and urbanisation process. Cities in wealthy regions grew as a result of migration from poorer areas in search of work and better living conditions.

However, due to the disordered growth of the poor population, for reasons of hygiene and health, the demands took on proportions that went beyond care itself to the establishment of the organisation of time and space so that the child could be educated and, over the years, schooled.

But in order for this reality to take hold, processes involving government and civil bodies took place over the decades, for example, in the 1920s the state and the government provided tax incentives for childcare, as well as providing furniture, teaching staff and staff for this care, however, the aim was to "support" the working family in the sense that if the child was well, the worker would work happily (SANCHES, 2003).

With the Consolidation of Labour Laws (CLT) in 1943, nurseries appeared, but to guarantee the mother's right to breastfeed her child, and during this period, with regard to crèches, "they were part of a policy to protect maternity and childhood, linked to the areas of health and social assistance [...]" according to Sanches (2003, p. 66).

Still according to the author, in this period kindergartens existed for educational purposes, unlike crèches, which were not concerned with educating children, but rather with assisting them. In this context, home-based crèches and other possibilities for childcare also emerged, as structural demands had eased, although problems such as infant mortality and malnutrition had arisen (ibid., p. 67).

The 1970s were a significant decade in terms of the conquest for crèches to meet the needs of the labour community, where women were predominant. This presence also became notorious in organisations and demands for better care for children. During this period, and more precisely "in October 1978, the Movement of Struggles for Crèches was officially launched, which expanded, especially in large urban centres (SANCHES, 2003, p. 69).

It was against this backdrop that the education of young children became something serious and led to "[...] a movement by civil society and government bodies to have the care of children from zero to six years recognised in the 1988 Federal Constitution," according to Brasil (1988, p. 11).

Since then, the guarantee of education has been constituted as a social right and a duty of the State, and is included in the country's magna carta - the Federal Constitution of 1988, assuring children in the following terms: "nursery and pre-school care for children from zero to six years of age", according to item IV of Article 208 of Section I of Chapter III. (BRASIL, 1988, p. 35).

The Constitution then became the milestone for the Law of Guidelines and Bases for National Education (LDBEN), under Law 9.394, of 20 December 1996, to establish in Title V, Chapter II, Section II of Art. 29 that "Early Childhood Education is considered the first stage of basic education" according to what is stated in Brasil (2015, p. 22). As such, this stage aims to promote the all-round development of children up to the age of six.

Following the establishment of Early Childhood Education as an integral part of Basic Education in 1998, the National Curriculum Framework for Early Childhood Education (RECNEI) was delivered to the professional public in this segment, as a reflective and guiding instrument for actions with objectives, content and teaching guidelines to assist in teaching practice regarding the development of children in their educational environment (BRASIL, 1998).

In 2009, Resolution No. 5 of 17/12 established the National Curriculum Guidelines for Early Childhood Education (DECNEI), presenting conceptions of the child, the curriculum and the pedagogical proposal for Early Childhood Education, as well as the organisation of space and time, among many other aspects pertinent to the child. One of its aims is to "[...] guide public policies and the development, planning, implementation and evaluation of pedagogical and curricular proposals for Early Childhood Education." (BRASIL, 2010)

The Common National Base (BNCC), still being formulated in the current year, consolidates the achievements of the Guidelines and thus designates a curricular organisation for Early Childhood Education. Based on the child's experiences, the BNCC promotes the appropriation of relevant knowledge considering the five aspects: The self, the other and the we; Body, gestures and movements; Strokes, sounds, colours and images; Listening, speech, language and thought; Spaces, times, quantities, relationships and transformations. (BRASIL, 2016)

Given that children are recognised from an early age as citizens with rights, it is also important to add to this that support for their education is also established, with the same wording as the Constitution, in Article 54 (IV) of the Statute of the Child and Adolescent (ECA). This document aims to provide comprehensive protection for children and adolescents, considering them to be fully developing beings.

Narrowing in on Special Education, it is important to add that according to Rosa and Dutra (2016):

> Although this initiative can be considered a step forward, it is important to note that modern special education was born as part of the movement to democratise and universalise education. A process undertaken by the bourgeoisie against the privileges and perks of the nobility, alongside the extension of schooling to children who, due to personal characteristics, were unable to benefit from regular education processes.

However, a long historical process - between struggles and laws - has been established so that children who need Special Education are in fact catered for. Thus, Article 208(III) and Article 54 of the Federal Constitution and the ECA, respectively, ensure in their terms that Special Education must be granted and supported: "[...] preferably in the regular education network." (BRASIL, 2014, p. 1). (BRASIL, 2014, p. 33). However, the service referred to has not been legally complied with in the regular public education networks in São Luís.

It's worth noting that, just like early childhood education, special needs education has undergone a process of public and educational policy to be recognised as paramount. In addition, from 7 to 10 June 1994, the "[...] World Conference on Special Educational

Needs was held in Salamanca, Spain, under the patronage of UNESCO and the Spanish Ministry of Education and Science [...]" according to the text in Brasil (2006, p. 18). Its line of action is based on

> [...] in the experience of the participating countries and also in the resolutions, recommendations and publications of the United Nations system and other intergovernmental organisations, especially the Uniform Standards on Equal Opportunities for Persons with Disabilities. (BRASIL, 2006, p. 18).

Given the legal context presented, it is now time to present what the LDBEN defines as Special Education, which is aimed at people with disabilities.

> Art. 58 - For the purposes of this Law, Special Education is understood to be the type of school education offered preferentially in the regular school network for students with disabilities, global development disorders and high abilities or giftedness. (BRASIL, 2015, p. 34)

The regular education system, especially public schools, is permeated by difficulties of all kinds: administrative, structural, pedagogical and others. If we look at those who fall within the definition of Special Education, it makes teaching much more challenging, since their specificities will not be catered for in the way regulated by law. And, in terms of inclusive education, Special Education"[...] permeates the levels, stages and modalities of education" according to the writings of Brasil (2016). These writings also state that:

> School inclusion precepts and ensures the fulfilment of everyone's right to education, rejecting the educational proposals of schools based on the paradigm that conceives of people as ready-made products designed according to a unified educational model (BRASIL, 2016).

It can therefore be inferred that inclusion precepts the value of difference. A difference that for many years has ensured that only a few have the right to formal education, given that historically education has perpetuated the inclusion/exclusion framework according to the current social dictates that have always proclaimed knowledge for an economically favoured slice of the population, reflected in the same way of reproduction for those who are socially considered different.

Lastly, the legal framework for Special Education is specifically regulated by Law 13.146 of 6 July 2015. This law, also established as the Statute of Persons with Disabilities, ensures and promotes, on equal terms, the exercise of fundamental rights and freedoms for people with disabilities, with a view to their citizenship and social inclusion (BRASIL, 2015).

The aim is to make it possible for citizens with disabilities to have their rights considered and effectively granted, especially with regard to education, given that their integration into society and the labour market will depend on their acceptance into society as a whole.

2.1 Terminology in Learning and Special Education: a necessary understanding

2.1.1 Learning

It would be too much of a pretence to present anything in depth about learning itself in this chapter, given its specificities, which are just as broad and complex as those of Special Needs Education.

However, it is considered pertinent to address both learning and Special Education for three reasons: the first because learning, for the most part, depends on the perfect functional development of the brain, this being the underlying organ of cognition and the other functions of the human body; the second, because of the universe of peculiarities that has entered the classrooms, one might say, in the last two decades in order to meet the laws that determine equal care for any and all citizens, especially with regard to education; and the third: because this universe - the learner, is the subject of learning and thus the greatest challenge of/for a teacher.

Although Special Education was legally formalised in Brazil in the 20th century, according to the writings of Relvas (2015, p. 56) the "[...] interest in special pedagogical care for children with school difficulties dates back to the mid-1500s by Ponce Leon in Spain, author of the first pedagogical essays for the deaf and dumb."

It was in this context and in continuity with it that Pestalozi and Montessori developed means and methods of learning using sensory mechanisms such as intuitive and concrete education, and the power of self-education through the child's freedom of action, respectively. Other educators such as Dewey also paid attention to children who had certain learning difficulties (RELVAS, 2015).

Now, learning is something that is essential and that occurs gradually and on a daily basis. The environments in which the child is inserted, in other words, the family, the school, society, all contribute to this, although for some there are physical, psychological and functional barriers that prevent it from taking place. According to Relvas (2015) the:

> Learning difficulties encompass a heterogeneous group of problems capable of altering a child's ability to learn, regardless of their neurological conditions for doing so. The term learning disorders should be reserved for primary or specific difficulties in CNS alterations (RELVAS, 2015, p. 58-59).

In other words, formal learning may or may not take place, or it may take place slowly, sometimes involving physical, emotional, cognitive and family issues, among others. These aspects can trigger problems such as disorders or syndromes, which can also be physiological, biological or emotional, and which have directly affected the development and learning of children and adolescents in the last century.

Learning difficulties have become so important that the Brazilian Psychiatric Association (ABP) developed the Diagnostic and Statistical Manual of Mental Disorders (DSM-5). For other areas of health that in one way or another develop work or diagnoses for education, they use the International Code of Diseases (ICD-10). Both of these list the problems presented here as being amenable to medical monitoring and treatment, sometimes under drug conditions.

As far as learning is concerned, there are disorders that are known as Specific Learning Disorders (SLD). Cosenza and Guerra (2011, p. 132) state that learning disorders are examples of genetically determined alterations in specific brain circuits that directly interfere with the acquisition of skills such as reading, writing and logical-mathematical reasoning. The authors estimate that, depending on how they are assessed, they affect between 2 and 10 per cent of the population.

They are conditions that "comprise a specific inability, such as reading, writing or maths, in individuals who show results that are significantly below those expected for their level of development and intellectual capacity." (RELVAS, 2015, p. 53).

According to Gómez and Terán (2009), Specific Learning Disorders (SLD):

> [...] they imply a performance in the academic area below that expected for the age, intellectual level and educational level, the manifestations of which extend to the other areas of life only in those aspects that require reading, writing or calculation.

Gómez and Terán (2009) point out that these disorders should not be confused with disabilities because they directly affect actions such as spelling, writing, remembering and organising, among others. Furthermore, they can also be considered a sign of behavioural decompensation, as they do not constitute a permanent condition and can be reversed by recognising this reality and working on it in a specific way.

For Gómez and Terán (2009), these disorders include dyscalculia, dyslalia, dysgraphia and others. Relvas (2015) uses the same terms and considers them to be language-related disorders, classifying them as follows: reading - alexia and dyslexia, total inability or insufficient mastery of reading, respectively; writing - agraphia, dysgraphia, dysorthography, dyscaligraphy, dyssyntax and mirror writing; arithmetic - acalculia, dyscalculia (mental or graphic), and are respectively total inoperability or partial difficulty in maths.

According to Cosenza and Guerra (2011) dyslexia is a "neurobiological disorder characterised by difficulty in the accurate or fluent recognition of words, with difficulty in spelling and recoding graphic signs into sounds." The authors also state that 80% of those diagnosed with dyslexia are in fact dyslexic.

Dyscalculia is the other most commonly diagnosed disorder. In this case, the child is unable to grasp the concept of number, making everything related to maths more difficult. "The causes of dyscalculia are not yet known, but there seems to be an alteration in the circuits of the parietal lobe, caused by early injury or a genetic defect at the time of its formation," say Cosenza and Guerra (2011, p. 114).

It's interesting to note that in addition to learning disorders, there are also mental and behavioural disorders which, in one way or another, also influence learning. When dealing with these types of disorders, Ballone (2008) bases himself on what has been established by the World Health Organisation - WHO:

> [...] Mental and Behavioural Disorders are conditions characterised by morbid alterations in thinking and/or mood (emotions), and/or morbid alterations in behaviour associated with expressive distress and/or deterioration in overall psychological functioning. Mental and Behavioural Disorders are not just variations on the "normal" scale, but clearly abnormal or pathological phenomena.

According to Ballone (2008), disorders can be developmental (mental retardation); global developmental disorders (autistic spectrum); anxiety disorders; behavioural disorders (ADHD - attention deficit/hyperactivity disorder, CT - conduct disorder, ODD - oppositional defiant disorder); tic disorders (Tourette's or TS); excretory disorders (encopresis or functional enuresis); eating disorders (rumination); psychiatric disorders (depression, dysthymia, etc.); bipolar disorder, among many others that are subdivided depending on the degree (mild, moderate and severe).

Of the disorders mentioned, the most common in the classroom is ADHD. This is a disorder that usually manifests itself in childhood, although it is not diagnosed before the age of three. It lasts into adulthood, affects individuals of both sexes and is considered chronic. This disorder is characterised by altered emotional control, inappropriate impulsivity, attention problems and hyperactivity, as well as difficulty socialising (COSENZA E GUERRA, 2011).

The authors also state that there are subtypes of ADHD, which are: predominantly inattentive, predominantly hyperactive-impulsive and combined (ibid., p. 136).

Another important aspect to mention is syndromes. These, in turn, according to Cancino (2015) "are a set of relatively frequent signs and symptoms that tend to present in groups for certain individuals and that allow a population to be defined as having or being affected by such a condition."

Ballone (2008) states that the syndromes include: Angelman, Asperger, Balint, Burnout, Ganser, Kluver-Bucy, Korsakoff, Wernicke, Frontal Lobe, Down's, Munchausen, Nolitiva, Panic Disorder, Restless Legs and Fragile X syndrome. Most of these syndromes are triggered by genetic problems and cause or influence mental retardation.

Relvas (2015) also introduces us to other types of syndromes such as Edwards' Syndrome, Patan's Syndrome, Turner's Syndrome, Klinefelter's Syndrome, Down's Syndrome and Fragile X Syndrome. The author also discusses genetic syndromes, emphasising that it is vital for teachers to identify characteristics in their students that are present in the head, hands and feet. The author states that syndromes are the result of:

> [...] alterations in foetal development, present since fertilisation, located either in the chromosomes (chromosomopathies) or in the genes (genetic diseases). They determine physical and/or biochemical changes in the foetus, which will remain for life, from the embryo to old age. (RELVAS, 2015, p. 102)

The disorders and syndromes presented here certainly don't represent a third of the existing reality affecting school-age children. Whether they realise it or not, families can strive for their children's success or fail to accept these circumstances, causing the child's development to be delayed.

According to Cosenza and Guerra (2011, p. 130) "it is estimated that learning difficulties, related to various causes, occur in 15 to 20 per cent of children in the first year of school and can reach higher numbers in the first six years of school", i.e. this rate refers to children in Early Childhood Education.

Having dealt with learning difficulties, we move on to Special Education and its terminology.

2.1.2 Special Education

Education for people with disabilities, until a certain point in history and more precisely until the 18th century, was treated on the basis of mysticism and the occult, since there was no scientific basis to corroborate a better analysis, enabling a certain marginalisation and/or people with such specificities to be ignored. The church also exerted a certain influence in this sense, because by placing man in the condition of "image and likeness of God" it conditioned the human being to accept perfection in the physical and mental sense (MAZZOTA, 2005).

But it was with the blind and the deaf, in past contexts, that it all began. In 1620, Jean-Paulo Bonet's "Letters and the Art of Teaching the Dumb to Speak" recorded the first printed work for deaf-mutes. In 1770, the first institution for deaf mutes was founded in Paris by the abbot Charles M. Eppée, and he was the creator of the sign method. The Englishman Thomas Braidwood (1715-1806) and the German Heinecke (1729-1790), who founded institutes for the deaf and dumb in their respective countries, also stand out in terms of their treatment of the deaf and dumb (MAZZOTA, 2005).

Valentin Hauyque founded the Institute for Blind Youth in Paris in 1974. In 1829 Louis Braille (1809-1852), a student at the institute, realised the feat of adapting the military code of nocturnal communication to meet the needs of the blind, initially called sonography and later definitively changed to Braille. "To date, no other means of reading and writing has been found that is more efficient and useful for blind people. Based on six protruding dots on the braille cell, this 'code' allows for sixty-three combinations," according to studies by Mazzota (2005, p. 19).

But the attention deserved for special needs in general was echoed around the world by the Salamanca Declaration.

In order to comply with international agreements, under the terms of the law for Brazil specifically, Special Education was then conceptualised in Article 58 of Chapter V of LDBEN/96 as follows: "For the purposes of this law, Special Education is understood to be the type of school education, preferably offered in the regular school system, for students with special needs." (BRASIL, 2010, p. 43).

According to the National Policy on Special Needs Education from the Perspective of Inclusive Education (2007),

> [A person with a disability is one who has long-term physical, mental or sensory impairments which, in interaction with various barriers, may restrict their full and effective participation in school and society. Students with global development disorders are those with qualitative alterations in reciprocal social interactions and communication, a restricted, stereotyped and repetitive repertoire of interests and activities. This group includes students with autism, autism spectrum syndromes and childhood psychosis. Students with high abilities/gifted demonstrate high potential in any of the following areas, alone or in combination: intellectual, academic, leadership, psychomotor and arts, as well as showing great creativity, involvement in learning and carrying out tasks in areas that interest them. (BRASIL, 2007)

It's interesting to look at the text above when interpreted in schematic form in order to get an overview of the terms and how they can be subdivided given their scope.

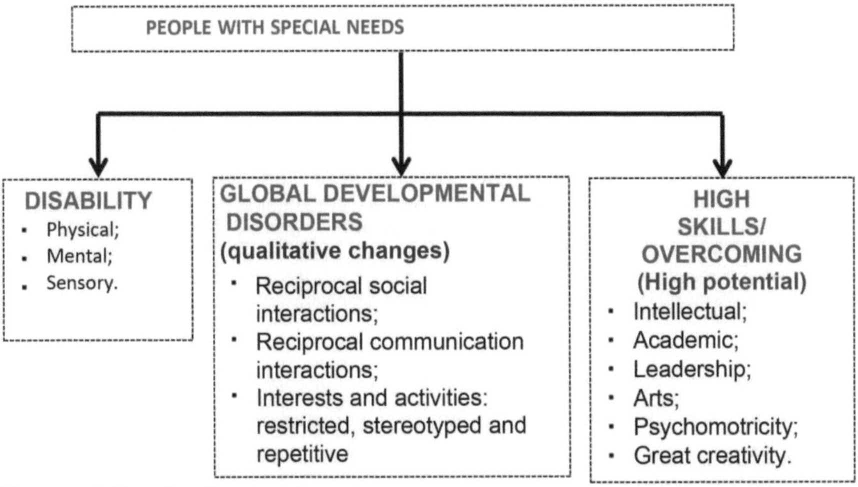

Diagram 1: People with special needs
Source: From the author.

The concept of disability was established in Section I of Article 3° of Decree No. 3.298 of 20 December 1999 in the following terms: "any loss or abnormality of a psychological, physiological or anatomical structure or function that generates incapacity for the performance of activity, within the standard considered normal for the human being". However, it is interesting to note that the universe of disabilities is much broader than one might imagine. The definitions of physical disabilities based on the **"disabled** online" website refer to

> [...] complete or partial alteration of one or more segments of the human body, leading to impairment of physical function, [...] limbs with congenital or acquired deformity, except for aesthetic deformities and those that do not produce difficulties for the performance of functions. (DISABLED..., 2016)

As for the types, they can be

Table 1: Types of physical disabilities

TYPE	DEFINITION
Paraplegia	Total loss of lower limb function.
Paraparesis	Partial loss of lower limb motor functions.
Monoplegia	Total loss of motor function of a single limb (lower or posterior).
Monoparesis	Partial loss of motor function in a single limb (lower or posterior).
Tetraplegia	Total loss of lower and upper limb motor functions.
Tetraparesis	Partial loss of lower and upper limb motor functions.
Triplegia	Total loss of motor functions in three limbs.
T riparesia	Partial loss of motor functions in three limbs.
Hemiplegia	Total loss of motor functions in one hemisphere of the body (right or left).
Hemiparesis	Partial loss of motor functions in one hemisphere of the body (right or left).

Amputation	Total or partial loss of a given limb or limb segment.
Cerebral palsy	Injury to one or more areas of the central nervous system, resulting in psychomotor alterations, which may or may not cause mental disability.
Ostomy	Surgical intervention that creates an ostoma (opening, ostium) in the abdominal wall for the adaptation of a collection bag; surgical process that aims to construct an alternative and new pathway for the elimination of faeces and urine to the outside of the human body, (colostomy: intestinal ostoma; urostoma; urinary diversion).

Source: The inclusion of the disabled person and the rehabilitated beneficiary in the labour market; MPT/Commission of Studies for the inclusion of the disabled person in the labour market - Brasília/DF - 2001. Available at: <http://www.deficienteonline.com.br/deficiencia- fisica-tipos-e-definicoes12 .html.> Accessed on: 13 Nov. 2016.

As far as mental disability is concerned, the concept itself has generated certain contradictions. The World Health Organisation (WHO), based on intelligence quotient (IQ), classifies mental retardation under codes F70 - F79 according to the International Code of Diseases (ICD-10).

Psychoanalysis is based on the conscious dimension dealt with by Freud in an attempt to define it, while developmental psychology takes a stance on the term without being able to define it either. Other authors, such as Lacan, deal with it by applying the term weak and being a pathology.

In this context, considerations of mental disability are considered antagonistic, and there is a difficulty in "[...] establishing a differential diagnosis between mental illness (which includes diagnoses of psychosis and early psychosis) and mental disability, especially in the case of young school-age children." (BRASIL, 2017, p. 15).

The American Association on Mental Disability (AAMD) states that:

> It manifests itself before the age of 18 and is characterised by significantly below-average general intellectual functioning, with limitations associated with two or more areas of adaptive behaviour or the individual's ability to respond adequately to the demands of society (DIFFERENTES..., 2017).

And that it also comes in different levels, enabling the disabled person to carry out ordinary activities, although sometimes they need a certain amount of help. They are classified as mild, moderate, severe or profound.

When mild, the person is able to develop school and professional skills and even provide for themselves. In moderate cases, the individual has insufficient capacity for social development. Severe cases have limited motor development and minimal language development. Profound causes a preponderance of retardation and the sensory motor capacity is minimal.

> The diagnosis from the medical and psychological fields defines the mentally

> handicapped as: people who have psychological difficulties due to neurological organic pathologies. The origin of this organic pathology lies in a problematic pregnancy or difficult labour (DIFFERENTES..., 2017).

In this context, there is an indisputable relationship between physical illnesses that are directly linked to mental illnesses in the sense of those that directly affect the central nervous system, such as cerebral palsy. In addition to prominent physical limitations, cerebral palsy usually brings with it agitation, aggression, stereotypes (repetitive movements), lack of hygiene habits, inappropriate and bizarre behaviour, as well as behavioural disorders caused by "[...] intellectual disability, epilepsy, sensory disorders [...]", as well as sleep disorders (MAIA, 2001, p. 45).

Still on the subject of disabilities, let's move on to sensory disabilities. These are divided into visual impairment and hearing impairment. Visual impairment or blindness "is a severe or total alteration of one or more of the elementary functions of vision that irreparably affects the ability to perceive colour, size, distance, shape, position or movement in a more or less comprehensive field". (BRASIL, 2007, p. 15).

Blindness can be congenital or acquired - also known as adventitious and, respectively, it can exist from birth or occur later due to organic or accidental causes. It can also be considered monocular when it affects only one eye or it can affect both eyes - binocular. Blindness care includes people with low vision or:

> [...] (amblyopia, low vision or residual vision) is complex due to the variety and intensity of visual function impairments. These functions range from the simple perception of light to reduced acuity and visual field that interfere with or limit the execution of tasks and general performance (BRASIL, 2007, p. 16).

There are cases in which a person is considered deafblind because of the association between blindness and hearing loss. The absence or limitation of sight is an important condition for learning to take place, since experiences and relationships with the environment play a major role in the acquisition and internalisation of concepts, orientation and mobility. "Vision, also known as the sense of distance, is the only perception capable of providing global contact with the environment. It is estimated that 80 to 85 per cent of the learning process depends on vision," adds Costa (2011, p. 53).

As for the definition of hearing impairment, Costa (2011) states that it is "considered generically as the difference between the individual's *performance* and the normal ability to detect sound according to the standards established by the American National Standards Institute."

Hearing problems include hypoacusis - a reduction in hearing sensitivity; dysacusis - a hearing disorder affecting sound quality rather than sound intensity;

conductive hearing loss - the inner ear is not stimulated by sound vibration; sensorineural hearing loss - Irreversible, as it occurs when there is damage to the hair cells of the cochlea or the auditory nerve, making it impossible to receive sound; Mixed hearing impairment - when sound is altered at the moment of conduction due to damage to the sensory organ, and central hearing impairment (central deafness) - refers to the difficulty of understanding sound information when processing sound information in the brainstem or auditory cortex. (COSTA, 2011, p. 55-56).

When it comes to Global Developmental Disorders, it's worth pointing out that it was covered when the types of disorders that directly or indirectly affect learning were defined and cited, but it's important to draw attention now when the law mentions "child psychosis" and includes it among the disorders. This, in turn, is understood by Tengan and Maia (2004):

> It can be defined as a mental disorder in which thinking, affective response and the ability to perceive reality are compromised. In addition to these symptoms, interpersonal relationships are usually severely impaired, which substantially interferes with social interaction. The classic characteristics of psychosis are: impaired ability to perceive reality adequately, the presence of delusions, hallucinations and illusions.

In their article, the authors add the peculiar and important fact that, up to a certain point, some psychoanalytic authors still considered childhood autism to be a chronic psychotic condition.

It is therefore important to add that psychosis is divided into conditions that are considered acute or chronic. Acute and recurrent psychoses are also known as cycloid psychosis; there are also substance-induced psychoses or acute organic psychoses. Chronic psychoses include schizophrenia, schizoaffective disorder, schizophreniform disorder and persistent delusional disorder (TENGAN and MAIA, 2004).

When it comes to differentiating between what is a chronic or acute condition, Ferreira (2010), when dealing with the terms according to medicine, "it is said of long-term illnesses, as opposed to those with an acute manifestation."

Finally, the law introduces high abilities. Until a certain point in history, children and adolescents who stood out from their peers for intellectual and/or cognitive reasons had their abilities measured by the IQ (Intelligence Quotient).

By the 1950s, what had been established as genius was broadened by the work of J.P. Guilford, who demonstrated that it was possible for some people to have a greater power both to solve complex problems and to be creative (ANTUNES, 2008).

Research and studies over the decades and with significant advances in science have enabled new, safer conceptions, as well as broadening the understanding of those in the classroom. Still according to Antunes (2008), "the work of the teacher in the area of high abilities translates into a *permanent challenge and requires a posture of permanent facilitator 'of the learning process'."* (Ibidem, p. 73).

Therefore, when it comes to special education and inclusion, it is important to understand what is considered normal and/or pathological, as well as what constitutes a disorder and a syndrome, among other aspects that are imbued in the issues surrounding special education, since they directly affect the individual, whether physically, biologically, psychologically and/or cognitively, making it extremely complex, including in and for the realisation of learning. From this perspective, Goffredo (1999, p. 70) defends the idea that, "considering teacher training for inclusive special education, content relating to conceptualisation, i.e. the typology of disabilities, should be part of the curriculum".

The point of all this was to show that the educational demand itself is extremely demanding in terms of the individual's learning and, in this process, it is up to the teacher to get to know their students, create bonds and make efforts to ensure that learning takes place. They have to look for ways and means, methods and didactics that make the student succeed and remain attentive to the applied content, but what can be done in the face of the extensive list of disorders, syndromes, disabilities and other particularities that, associated or not, make up the body of specificities that Special Education must encompass in order to meet the requirements of the law? What means, resources and time?

What is certain is that we are in fact falling short of being able to provide significant assistance to those who need specialised care, especially when it comes to regular education.

2.2 The process of including young children with disabilities, global developmental disorders and high abilities/giftedness

When it comes to the early history of education for children with disabilities, it's important to emphasise that it was carried out in special schools, which led to segregation, as they were often considered incapable of living with children seen as normal who were enrolled in regular education, today known as the ordinary classroom.

According to Aranha (2005, p. 21), "the concept of inclusion involves the same assumption as that of integration, namely the right of people with special educational needs to equal access to the common space of life in society", as it was once uncommon to find special students in regular classrooms, although their presence in public schools is currently timid.

However, researcher Rosita Edler Carvalho presents inclusion and integration differently. For the author, school integration is "[...] a process of educating/teaching so-called normal children together with children with disabilities, for part or all of their time at school." (CARVALHO, 1999, p. 36).

She assures us that this process of integration can only run the risk of inserting these students into the life of others without actually interacting, and that initiatives are needed from everyone involved, not just specialised educators, because there needs to be a change in attitude towards difference and non-rejection.

With regard to inclusive education, the author states that it has been conceptualised "[...] as a process of educating together and in an unconditional manner, in ordinary school classes, so-called normal pupils with pupils - with or without disabilities - who have special educational needs." (CARVALHO, 1999, p. 38).

Still on the subject of inclusive education, and based on the concept presented, the author believes that it is the ideal to hope for a world in which "[...] co-operation does not have the moral presupposition of pity, which generates benevolence" (Idem), and all of this as an integral part of the right to citizenship.

Discussions about inclusion in all social segments have always been of great importance, taking on much greater proportions in recent decades and, given the difficulties of the context, it's important to add that meetings aimed at this audience have been crucial to the advances that are currently taking place. In this respect, Biaggio (2007, p. 20) points out that:

> These include the World Declaration on Education for All, the result of the World Education Conference held in Jomtien, Thailand, in 1990, and later the Salamanca Declaration, from the World Conference on Special Needs Education: Access and Quality (UNESCO, 1994).

In order to avoid further prejudice and segregation, it was necessary to adapt the term that refers to them and, by means of Ordinance 2.344 of 3 November 2010, the term "people with disabilities" was established, given that they used to be called "people with disabilities" as they were in the initial texts of the laws. It should also be added that the change was due to the United Nations (UN) Convention on the Rights of Persons with Disabilities.

When it comes to the entry of children with disabilities into mainstream education, it is worth noting that this attitude was made possible by the United Nations, which reaffirmed,

> [...] the rights recognised in the Declaration of the Rights of the Child of 1959, as well as in the Beijing Rules of 1985, the Convention on the Rights of the Child (1989), the United Nations Rules for the Protection of Juveniles Deprived of their Liberty

> (1990) and the United Nations Guidelines for the Prevention of Juvenile Delinquency (Riyadh Guidelines - 1990). (CINTRA, 2008, p. 41).

Therefore, although child protection is addressed internationally, it is through the Statute of the Child and Adolescent (ECA, 1990) that Brazil establishes the guarantee of rights pertaining to children and adolescents, including education as an accessibility for all, regardless of their physical condition.

Among the laws, decrees and opinions, on 2 October 2009 Resolution No. 4 was ratified, establishing Operational Guidelines for Specialised Educational Assistance in Basic Education, Special Education modality, in the following terms:

> Art 1º In order to implement Decree 6.571/2008, education systems must enrol students with disabilities, global development disorders and high abilities in ordinary regular education classes and in Specialised Educational Assistance (AEE), offered in multifunctional resource rooms or in Specialised Educational Assistance centres in the public network or in non-profit community, confessional or philanthropic institutions.

However, the concept of special education from the perspective of inclusive education was also the result of social movements, because the laws that support children with disabilities in ordinary classrooms did not always guarantee this access, but the search for specialised care continued.

According to Craveiro's (2013) report on CNE/CEB Opinion No. 13/2009, the provision of ESA should be planned and carried out in the opposite shift to that of schooling, as students are guaranteed their education because they are attending both the regular class and specialised care.

Even with the guarantee of technical and financial assistance, as established by Decree 6.571/2008, the absence of children in resource rooms has prevailed, but the search for an effective guarantee remains, and it is worth noting that in the last decade an important insight has been gained into the aspects of the National Guidelines for Human Rights Education.

From the achievements in the field of inclusive education, it is important to note that Special Education has as its target group students with physical, sensory and intellectual disabilities. There are also students with global development disorders (including autism, Asperger's syndrome, among others) and students with high abilities.

Among the particularities of special education in the mainstream classroom, the teacher is still faced with children who have attention deficits, problems such as dysgraphia, dyslalia, dyslexia, among many others, which make this profession a challenging one, especially when looking at children in early childhood education, which in itself demands essential and necessary care.

According to Biaggio (2007), the MEC mobilised itself to serve the target public of Special Education through the Inclusive Education Programme, which was designed for basic education, including Early Childhood Education.

> The programme provides education systems with equipment, furniture and teaching materials to set up resource rooms and organise the provision of services. It has also implemented a number of other actions and programmes in partnership with state and municipal education managers, as well as supporting continuing teacher training in various areas, such as Mental Disability, Hearing Disability, Visual Disability, Giftedness/High Abilities, among others. (BIAGGIO, 2007, p. 21)

The proposal was to train managers and teachers so that this public could be successfully reached in terms of education and access to it. However, no documents have been found that reaffirm the development and finalisation of the process and show the final results.

In the 2007 article, the focus was on moving and mobilising the community in general to accept children with disabilities in mainstream education in order to comply not only with the law, but also to seek transformations in the curriculum, the pedagogical policy project and the practices of both management and classroom teachers. As Chahini (2010, p. 36) sees it, "the process of inclusion not only challenges educational systems in all their forms, but also society as a whole."

It is known in practice, taking as an example the regular public school network in São Luís - the one that encompasses Early Childhood Education - that there are recurrent complaints about the physical structure available - when it exists - for disabled children. Similarly, professional qualifications fall short of what is expected to cater for, include and actually teach a child with such specificities.

CHAPTER 3

THE PEDAGOGUE'S QUALIFICATION FROM THE PERSPECTIVE OF INCLUSION

Etymologically, the word Pedagogue originates from the "word *paidagogos* literally meaning the one who leads the child (agogós, "who leads") [...]" as Aranha (1996, p. 41) corroborates and has been established since Ancient Greece. Over the years, this meaning has become so relevant and widespread that it has come to designate the entire theory of education.

The Pedagogy course was established at the end of the 1930s and "[...] was the result of a long process of attempts by legislators to define the basis for teacher training, especially for secondary education". (CRUZ, 2011, p. 30).

Its legal framework was established by Decree-Law No. 1190/39, dated 4 April 1939, with the organisation of the National Faculty of Philosophy, establishing Philosophy, Science, Literature and Pedagogy courses in sessions.

With the Decree, to become a pedagogue, it was enough to take two subjects, adding another one-year course, namely Didactics, which was called the "3+1 scheme". According to Deimling (2013), "in the curriculum model implemented by Decree No. 1190/39, there were no subjects specifically related to Special Education in the training of pedagogues".

The Pedagogy Course, given the structure mentioned above, trained bachelors and graduates, with the latter being granted the right to "[...] act as teachers at the Normal School, responsible for training primary teachers." (CRUZ, 2011, p. 36).

According to Cruz (2011), CFE Opinion No. 251 of 1962 is the second legal milestone for the Pedagogy course, in terms of establishing the minimum curriculum and the duration of the course, although it was only for the bachelor's degree, and he adds that "this opinion, authored by counsellor Valnir Chagas, was accompanied by a CFE Resolution, approved during the validity of LDB No. 4.024, of 21 December 1961, to take effect from 1963."

As for bachelor's degrees, their subjects were established in CFE Opinion No. 292 of 14 November, also drafted by Valnir Chagas. This opinion also abolished the "3+1 scheme". (CRUZ, 2011)

The University Reform came with Law No. 5.540, of 28 November 1968, which enabled new regulations for the Pedagogy course. According to Deimling (2013) "[...] carried out by CFE Opinion No. 252/69, which resulted in CFE Resolution No. 2/69, which set the contents and duration of the Pedagogy course." However, training was given for normal teaching, and specialisations were also granted in administration, supervision and school inspection. Once again, there was no specialisation in Special Education.

It is interesting to add that,

> This regulation maintained the training of teachers for Normal Education and officially introduced qualifications to train specialists responsible for planning, supervision, administration and guidance, which from then on became a strong means of identifying the pedagogue. (CRUZ, 2011, p. 47)

It was only at the end of the 1970s and beginning of the 1980s that there was a possibility of change due to the various criticisms that the course suffered, triggering a process of reformulation. Seminars and conferences arose from the criticism, and in 1990 the National Association for the Training of Education Professionals (ANFOPE) was formed. It was through ANFOPE's influence that the qualifications were abolished and the aim was to "[...] work predominantly with teacher training, including that of the initial grades of primary school."° (CRUZ, 2011, p. 49)

Still based on the records of Cruz (2011), the author designates CNE Resolution No. 1 of 10 April 2006 as the fourth legal framework for the Pedagogy course, since it is through this that the Curricular Guidelines for the Pedagogy Course are established, which is of significant importance in terms of the training of education professionals.

It wasn't until 1972 that something focused on Special Education emerged, although only the mentally handicapped were catered for. This initiative "was taken by the Pestalozzi Faculty of Science, Education and Technology, in the municipality of Franca (SP)." (DEIMLING, 2013)

This initiative marked the beginning of a new approach to disabled people in the following years, and so the area spread to many other states and universities in terms of higher education in pedagogy, as well as including qualifications for audio-communication and visually impaired people (DEIMLING, 2013).

In 1996, the National Education Guidelines and Bases Law (LDB) - Law No. 9.394 of 20 December 1996 - was approved, and its articles 61 to 67 deal specifically with the levels of professional training for basic education. According to Libâneo, Oliveira and Toschi (2012, p. 276):

> According to these articles, teacher training for basic education must be carried out in higher education courses with a full degree, with a minimum of secondary level training, in the normal modality, being admitted for the exercise of teaching in Early Childhood Education and in the four initial series of primary education [...].

In dealing with Special Education, the LDBN/96 in its Chapter V - Special

Education, Article 59 and Item III establishes that teachers must have "[...] appropriate specialisation at secondary or higher level, for specialised care, as well as regular education teachers trained for the integration of these students in common classes." (BRASIL, 2015, p. 34).

In 2001, CNE/CP Opinion No. 9/2001 approved the inclusion in basic education in the following terms: "Basic education must be inclusive, in the sense of meeting a policy of integrating students with special educational needs into the ordinary classes of the education systems." (BRASIL, 2001, p. 26)

Also in 2001, the National Education Plan (PNE) was approved, another extremely important document in terms of the inclusion of special needs students in mainstream education. It states that:

> The Federal Constitution establishes the right of people with special needs to receive education preferably in the regular school system (art. 208, III). The current guideline is the full integration of these people into all areas of society. It is therefore a question of two issues - the right to education, common to all people, and the right to receive this education whenever possible together with other people in "regular" schools. (BRASIL, 2001)

The following year - 2002 - two extremely important resolutions were passed, both in terms of teacher training and the fact that this training should include knowledge about students with special needs: CNE/CP Resolution No. 1/2002, which establishes the National Curriculum Guidelines for the Training of Basic Education Teachers, and CNE/CP Resolution No. 2/2002, which establishes the duration and workload of degree courses.

It is in this context that the qualification of the professional pedagogue has undergone transformations in line with the educational reforms that have taken place in previous and current decades because, according to Brandão (2007, p. 26), formal education is necessarily "[...] the moment when education becomes subject to *pedagogy* (the theory of education), creates its own situations for its exercise, produces its methods, establishes its rules and times, and constitutes specialised executors".

And so, in 2002, with the promulgation of CNE/CP Resolution No. 1/2002, from an inclusive education perspective, it was established that "higher education institutions should provide in their curricular organisation teacher training aimed at attention to diversity that includes knowledge about the specificities of students with SEN." (DEIMLING, 2013)

Over the years, mobilisations among researchers, unions, student bodies and associations have collapsed in discussions about the organisation and title of the Pedagogy course.

This reality led to the formation of the Bicameral Commission, from which came

CNE/CP Opinion No. 5/2005, which laid the foundations for the construction of the National Curriculum Guidelines for undergraduate courses in Pedagogy (DEIMLING, 2013).

In 2006, by means of CNE/CP No. 1, the Pedagogy course "reclaimed for itself the training of teachers for Early Childhood Education and the initial years of Primary Education, in addition to the non-teaching functions of this professional," as Deimling (2013, p. 243) points out.

As far as Special Education is concerned, it is well known that the person who dealt with the small child who was part of the nursery and pre-school body was called a carer because of the assistance nature of this instance. However, in 2007 the nomenclature changed, as Cerisara (2002, p. 329) adds:

> [...] by 2007 all professionals who work directly with children in nurseries and pre-schools, whether they are called classroom assistants, pajens, child development assistants, or any other name, will be considered teachers and must have specific training in the area.

For Godoffredo (1999, p. 67), the inclusion paradigm makes it extremely important to think about the education of this public right from nursery school, which, according to the author, "[...] now requires teachers to have knowledge other than that which they received in their teacher training courses". (Ibidem, p. 68).

It is therefore important to point out that initial pedagogical training trains this professional to work in Basic Education to cater for the following audiences: children from zero to six years old (nursery and Early Childhood Education) and seven to nine years old (initial and final grades of primary education - 1º to 5º). In Early Childhood Education, the teacher must work with the child based on axes of experience, as established by the National Common Curriculum Base (BNCC), which is still under discussion at national level. In the past, this practice was guided by the National Curriculum Framework for Early Childhood Education (RECNEI):

> Its function is to contribute to early childhood education policies and programmes, socialising information, discussions and research, supporting the educational work of technicians, teachers and other early childhood education professionals and supporting state and municipal education systems. (BRASIL, 1998, p. 13)

As for the initial and final grades, they must cover all the subjects they are responsible for - history, geography, Portuguese, maths, science and so on. Godoffredo (1999, p. 67) believes that among the many classroom duties, as well as the structural difficulties that teachers face from an inclusive perspective, they must "always be prepared to adapt to the new situations that will arise within the classroom".

These children demand specific and pertinent care, and the teacher still ends up adopting the character of a carer. And although Early Childhood Education is about supporting and mediating the integral development of children, taking into account their childhood and the fact that they are children, it is believed that this character has been lost amid social demands for children to learn to read and write quickly. Early childhood education has been distorted.

Pedagogical training to meet the specific needs of the disabled is also covered in the Salamanca Declaration (2016) when it comes to information and research, with the following terms:

> Pre-professional training should provide all primary or secondary school pedagogy students with a positive orientation towards disability, thereby developing an understanding of what can be achieved in schools through the support services available in the locality.

However, in an article published in 2013, Rosalba Garcia points out in her wide-ranging research that, for some scholars, training is part of the state's educational reforms, in which teachers have to take on new competences due to social complexity, and they also have to take responsibility for their own professionalisation, through the individual search for training, but also for achieving the objectives and goals of the policy itself. Finally, it should be added that

> The model of care proposed by the current policy makes the special education teacher a multifunctional being, the name given to resource rooms that cater for all types of pupils in this modality. Michels (2011) considers that faced with the need to deal with such a wide range of tasks, which contrasts with the restriction of training based on activities and resources, the ESL teacher becomes a manager of learning resources. We believe that this loses the essence of teaching (GARCIA, 2013, p. 115).

Finally, although there has been a lot of progress on inclusive education, including the actions of the MEC, there is still a lot to be done in terms of teacher training. Bringing this reality to the Basic Education Units of São Luís do Maranhão, we think that we are falling short of what is expected, because if we have distorted Early Childhood Education itself, what do we not do with Special Education? Inclusion would require a separate study given the deficiencies in our municipality's public education system.

CHAPTER 4

THE METHODOLOGY APPLIED

An exploratory study was carried out with the aim of providing an approximate overview of a given fact (GIL, 2014).

This general view relates to the fact that pedagogues are not prepared to deal with children with special needs in early childhood education, as demonstrated in the data analysis chapter.

Although the universe or population of the public appointed to be interviewed is relevant in terms of its existence, a sample of eleven professional pedagogues was established from this universe to carry out the interview and, therefore, it can be inferred that sampling by typicality or intentionality was adopted, as Gil (2014, p. 94) states that this type "[...] consists of selecting a subgroup of the population that, based on the information available, can be considered representative of the entire population."

As for being exploratory, we sought to "[...] clarify and modify concepts and ideas, with a view to formulating more precise problems or researchable hypotheses for further studies [...]" as Gil (2014, p. 27) corroborates, mainly due to the fact that higher education courses, in this case, pedagogy, have undergone changes in their legal bases over the decades, but that for Special Education the attention is not deserved during the academic training period.

This aspect should be strongly considered in the course curriculum in order to meet the increasing demand in the classroom.

Of the participants, seven are from public schools and four from public schools, with a degree in Pedagogy and who work in Early Childhood Education in the municipality of São Luís - MA. It should be noted that five have specialised in Psychopedagogy and that one of these five has also specialised in Special Education. In order to analyse the subjects' statements and preserve their identities, coding was used with an acronym followed by an Arabic number in ascending order as follows: P - Teacher (P1 to P11).

For data collection, non-participant observation and semi-structured interviews were used using a script containing 7 open questions. After the necessary clarifications to the participants, the questions were recorded and later transcribed for tabulation and analysis of the results. For tabulation, the statistical method of relative frequency distribution was used.

CHAPTER 5

RESULTS, ANALYSIS AND DISCUSSION

This chapter presents the results obtained from the interviews with the research participants, as well as the necessary analyses and discussion.

Of the eleven participants (100%), five have a specialisation in Psychopedagogy (45%) - P2, P3, P6, P8 and P11. The last one in the sequence, in addition to the specialisation mentioned, also has a specialisation in Special Education.

When asked about their **understanding of the target audience for Special Education,** 3 (27%) defended the idea that this is an audience that needs better care from teachers who are unprepared; 2 (18%) participants, because they work specifically in resource rooms (P3 and P11), said that they are children with a wide range of disorders, as well as Down's syndrome and autism; 2 (18%) reported that they were physically handicapped; 2 (18%) didn't define which public they were targeting, but said that it was a growing public in the education network; 1 (9%) believed that special education was too often confused with welfare and 1 (9%) believed that it was a public that needed adapted activities.

The results can be seen in the teachers' statements below:

> It's a public that should have more unique teaching, the participation of all the bodies and teachers who are dedicated especially to them, teaching that is done just for them, because the teachers are generally unprepared (PI);
> These are students who arrive with attention deficits, hyperactivity, motor coordination problems and need adapted activities (P2);
> This audience includes children with global disorders, Down's, autism, high abilities, deaf and visually impaired (P3);
> These are children with physical or cognitive disabilities who unfortunately don't have specialised people to work with them (P4);
> It's an area that isn't worked on, it's vague, it lacks direction. It's an audience that isn't reached with emphasis due to a lack of knowledge on the part of the teachers (P5);
> Our big argument in psycho-pedagogy is that special education is confused with welfare and there are not always priorities for it, or it is affected (P6);
> Special education encompasses everyone with a disability that prevents them from developing skills at home or in the classroom (P7);
> It's a growing audience with countless questions that involve family and school, bodies that need to be prepared (P8);
> These are children who end up growing up in the network and don't have the proper care to meet their needs (P9);
>
> Special Education today leaves us limited to everything we learnt in undergraduate courses, even the theory and practice leaves something to be desired (P10);
> These are children with disorders and high abilities. This is the target audience for Special Education (P11).

It can be seen that, in general, there is no concept or specific identification of this public, even by those who have a specialisation more focused on the area of Special

Education, such as Psychopedagogy (P2, P3, P6, P8 and P11), thus making the reports superficial when considering the essence of the question.

It is important to add that, although there is unanimity on the need for more in-depth qualifications for professional pedagogues so that this public can be effectively catered for, especially because of their specificities, these aspects have not been taken into account in the classroom, even though the number of children in this group is growing and they have arrived at the education network, regardless of whether it is private or public, without finding care that enables them to learn and, sometimes, develop.

Chahini (2010, p. 45) sees welfare as a problem for inclusion, as it is "[...] a real, logical and unavoidable need. And discrimination against students with disabilities is a violation of their right to education."

It is also worth mentioning what Antunes (2008) says about this reality. According to the author, the emergence of specialised schools for people with disabilities began in 1950. Before that, these children were ignored by the public authorities and the Brazilian education system. At a certain point, in order to demonstrate a certain recognition of the class, an education system was created, however, this was significantly segregationist to the point where special students were considered incapable.

There were two crucial and definitive moments for achieving real recognition for those considered to have been excluded until then. The first was the World Conference on Education for All held in Jomtien, Thailand in 1990. The second took place in Spain in 1994 with the drafting of the Salamanca Declaration on Principles, Policy and Practice in the Area of Special Needs Education (ANTUNES, 2008).

The fact is that in order to define who the target audience of Special Education is, one must consider the history and the long process that has taken place in the formation and structuring of this audience, and also that it is established from the concept of the term "special needs" disseminated after the Salamanca Declaration, which mentions it from an inclusive education perspective. Therefore, "[...] Special Education becomes part of the pedagogical proposal of the regular school, promoting the care of students with disabilities, global development disorders and high skills / giftedness." (BRASIL, p.11, 2007)

According to Antunes, these documents provided the basis for the pedagogy of inclusion from a legal point of view.

> However, for this to actually happen, it is necessary to recognise that inclusion implies a restructuring of schools and the need to implement a pedagogy geared towards diversity and the specific needs of students in different contexts. This shows that everything that has already been done represents a significant leap forward, but unfortunately it hasn't yet been realised (ANTUNES, 2008, p. 16).

With regard to the education of children with special needs, it is interesting to point out that the theory exists and has been reinforced in studies and research, but paradoxically, when it comes to practice, the reality is different. Most commonly, in both public and private networks, the student is in the regular classroom just to socialise, not finding in the classes and methods the means to contribute to their cognitive development and/or learning itself.

When asked about **their understanding of disability, global development disorders and high abilities,** the results had to be presented separately and as follows: 3 (27 per cent) related the three aspects as something that challenges teachers to seek more knowledge for their classroom practice, and these three should be considered for the sum of the eleven participants;

In terms of what a disabled person is, 6 (54 per cent) said that it was someone with limitations; 1 (10 per cent) said that it was something that hindered the child's cognitive development and the other 1 (10 per cent) said that it was something related to congenital issues.

As for what a disorder is, 4 (36 per cent) said it was a severe condition that hinders learning and the development of certain skills; 2 (18 per cent) said it was something to do with hyperactivity and attention deficit; 1 (10 per cent) said it was something to do with emotional factors and 1 (10 per cent) believed it was linked to biological and/or neurological issues.

When it comes to high abilities, 3 (27 per cent) participants said that it is someone who has greater ability in specific areas of knowledge; 2 (18 per cent) believe that it concerns those who are at a level above the rest of the class and 2 (18 per cent) immediately assured that it is a public without specific care or work aimed at them.

For a better understanding, the reports will follow the order of what is meant by people with disabilities, global developmental disorders and high abilities:

> When a person has something in their body or can't do something on their own and needs someone's help; something caused by a state of emotion outside the context of their life; people who, despite having a disorder, have a specific type of knowledge, a greater ability to do something (P1);
> It's when the child can't keep up with the other pupils and needs help in certain areas; they're children with attention deficits, hyperactivity; they're children who are at a higher level and the classroom activities are superficial (P2);
> Disability can be seen to be congenital. Nowadays, doctors can diagnose whether a child will be born with a disorder in the future through more advanced ultrasound scans. Through a more precise diagnosis and a multidisciplinary team, we can better understand, get to know and work on these disabilities followed by disorders (P3);
> There are various elements that get in the way of the teacher being resourceful in the classroom (P4);
> A child or adult who has limitations; When a child is born with a specific disability in reading or writing; When a child has an ease of learning, of understanding and is

> further ahead than others (P5);
> Disabilities and disorders differ but complement each other in the context of the child's development. They complement each other because they require stimuli from a different perspective on the part of the teacher. This also applies to those with high ability/gifted (P6);
> I see it as a problem that prevents a person from carrying out a certain task; it's related to the situation, to the severe conditions that also hinder the child from carrying out certain tasks; it's the ability to quickly resolve situations that are a little advanced for their age (P7);
> It's something that limits you; It's more linked to socialisation, communication, developing certain skills; Giftedness is a bigger challenge, it's a forgotten public (P8);
> It's anything that causes the child not to learn or even a physical problem that makes the child unable to learn. The school doesn't give accessibility, for example, to high ability. The school doesn't do specific work for them to develop and transform this high ability into growth (P9);
> It ends up being limitations that we have to learn to work with, to change ourselves as professionals, to relearn and redo everything that we have already learnt as undergraduates. Sensitise ourselves as human beings and put ourselves in the other person's shoes, in the family's shoes and even in the learner's shoes (P10);
> It's anything that limits a child from developing a skill, such as visual impairment; a disorder is linked to biological and neurological issues; and high ability is when a child has a knack for certain things, such as maths (P11).

From the reports, we can see that the interviewees had some difficulty interpreting and/or understanding what was actually asked. The others found it difficult to come up with an idea, a perception or a concept of what disability, global development disorders and high abilities/giftedness are.

As mentioned above, physical disability is a partial or total loss or abnormality of a limb that limits the individual from performing certain activities, but it should be noted that visual and hearing impairments are considered sensory disabilities.

With regard to global disorders, Gomes and Bosa (2004) corroborate the following concept:

> MDD encompasses Autistic Disorder, Rett Disorder, Childhood Disintegrative Disorder, Asperger's Disorder and Global Disorder without further specification. GDD is characterised by severe and global impairment in some areas of development, such as reciprocal social interaction skills, communication skills, the presence of stereotyped behaviours, interests and activities.

As for high abilities/gifted, these are those who "[...] have a high degree of potential in one or more areas of knowledge and human performance" according to Delou (2011, p. 72).

Based on the above, it can be inferred that, in general, the teachers interviewed find it difficult to define or establish any concept of the target audience of Special Education and this creates insecurity and uncertainty when working with them, although they are all always seeking information through studies and research in order to help their students in the classroom.

Regarding the question of academic background, **whether they have studied**

and

learnt about children considered to be the target audience of Special Education, in this case, children with disabilities, global development disorders and high abilities,? (63 per cent) said that although they had, it had been superficial, fragmented and that there had been a lot of theory without practice; 3 (27 per cent) participants were emphatic no; 1 (10 per cent) said yes, which can be seen from the responses below:

> No (P1);
> I had an isolated elective course. One year I had it and the next year it wasn't offered. It was during the specialisation that I studied a bit more (P2);
> The subject isn't detailed, it's given in a superficial way. In postgraduate courses in psychopedagogy it's covered a lot, but not in undergraduate courses (P3);
> Yes, but she hasn't learnt how to work with these children (P4);
> The subject of Special Education is very brief. It should be worked on more (P5);
> No (P6);
> Yes. Concepts, characteristics and how to identify them in the classroom (P7);
> Not at university. I studied on my own because I was already working with special children and didn't find any support at university (P8);
> Yes, I did. I took three courses in different periods on this subject, but it was all very theoretical and in practice it's nothing like what we learnt (P9);
> The only course in Special Education was very fragmented. Two or three pieces of literature, few moments of practice and experience. We visited the school for the blind and Libras once, there was a lottery and not everyone had access (P10);
> We had a course in Special Education, but the hours we studied it were very superficial. We didn't realise it was effective, we didn't see anything more in-depth in relation to Special Education (P11);

From the succinct "no" responses from P3, P5 and P9, who, although they have had Special Education subjects, are discouraged by the brevity and superficiality of the subject, as well as the fact that the theory doesn't match the practice.

We also realise that pedagogical training, whether public or private, is somewhat weak when it comes to Special Education. The curricular matrices of the courses in fact cover the subject of Special Education very superficially, and there is even a lack of time to delve deeper into the subject in view of the various difficulties that the teacher will encounter in the classroom, in addition to those dealt with here.

The issues surrounding Special Education deserve greater and better preparation in the sense of pedagogical training, this is a fact, but it has not been considered in its essence. The greatest detail and information, according to the interviewees, was acquired in the specialisation in Psychopedagogy and even so, in the face of all the questions, there is a certain hesitancy to conceptualise, to conceive of a particular concept. Theory, then, is extremely important, but contact and practice are more reassuring when dealing with a special person. As Antunes (2008) sees it

> The big problem with the countless learning disorders and difficulties we come across every day is much less in the pathology that characterises them and the lack of knowledge about how to identify them, and more in how to work with these students to help them think and learn.

In this sense, pedagogy is inherently and totally something much broader, more globalising. "It is a field of knowledge about the educational problem in its totality and historicity and, at the same time, a guideline for educational action," according to Libâneo (2010, p. 29-30).

When asked whether **during their undergraduate studies the content and workload allocated to Special Education were sufficient for their qualifications and/or for working with children considered to be the target audience of Special Education,** 11 (100%) considered that the workload and content were not sufficient to qualify and deal with Special Education. The following statements elucidate this information.

> No. It's very precarious (P1);
> Definitely not. When I was at university I had an elective course at the end of the term (P2);
> No. Before the MEC's formulation, it wasn't so emphatic (P3);
> No (P4);
> No. The chair should be wider (P5);
> No. So much so that when I started working I was given a child with Down's syndrome and I had to find ways of dealing with her (P6);
> I think the workload is insufficient. Special education is an area that needs special attention (P7);
> No (P8);
> No. Thirty hours and only theory is not enough. I can't deal with a child with just my degree (P9);
> It's not enough, it's too fragmented. Most of the information I have on how to deal and how to work has been acquired through extension courses, congresses and even continuing training courses where I work (P10);
> It wasn't enough. As for enabling, I've been looking for it on my own (P11).

As can be seen, the data shows unanimity in the "no, they are not insufficient" responses. Although the Pedagogy course has had its duration and workload established through CNE/CP Resolution No. 2/2002, nothing is defined about the subjects or a specific workload allocated to the education of those with special needs. In this sense, it is important to add the words of Silva (2015, p. 108):

> [...] a proposal for teacher training with a view to inclusive education must be understood as an integrated whole that involves the institutional project, the educational environments, the teaching materials, which are compatible with the needs and abilities of the students and enable conditions for effective quality of work for teachers and students.

As a relevant point, Freitas (2006) emphasises that one of the great challenges for degree courses is to design a curriculum that develops students' competences, skills and knowledge in relation to the teaching-learning process of students with specific educational needs.

For Godoffredo (1999), one of the aims of teacher training courses should be to create a "[...] critical awareness of the reality they will be working in and to provide them with a theoretical foundation that will enable them to take effective pedagogical action."

Therefore, the possibility of reviewing the hours and subjects that specifically address Special Education during academic training is essential, since the subjects that involve this public are generally 30 hours long, which makes it unfeasible to even get to know the many difficulties, disorders and problems that in one way or another directly interfere with the student's learning and development.

In relation to the **compulsory internships, if these were carried out in institutions that catered for children with disabilities, global developmental disorders and high abilities,** 6 (54%) participants said no; 2 (18%) said yes but without access to the children; 2 (18%) also said yes but without developing specific work in the classroom with these children and 1 (10%) reported yes but that it was a great challenge. According to the following statements:

> No (P1);
> No. At the time, I worked as a trainee with young people and adults and in the classrooms I worked in there were no disabled people (P2);
> No. The internship was focused on the regular classroom (P3);
> We had the internships but they weren't aimed at children with disabilities (P4);
> In the schools where I spent my internships, I didn't see any children with any of these types of disabilities, but the schools did have support rooms (P5);
> Yes, but there was also the question of not knowing how to work with that child. Then the child would... And, no, you don't worry about her because she's special and can just wander around the room. It's cruel (P6);
> No (P7);
> I did an internship at university. I had little access to children with disabilities, who were physically handicapped (motor) and mentally handicapped, and that really challenged me because I wasn't prepared to deal with them (P8);
> I even went to a school that had children with disabilities, but I didn't stay in any of the classrooms where they were (P9);
> I did have internships with children who had these disorders, but they didn't have the tutoring that we know is necessary in the classroom. They were left on the sidelines of the process, so they just occupied a place in the classroom (P10);
>
> No (P11).

In view of these facts, it is important to emphasise that the legal documents that establish pedagogical training for basic education have nothing specific to say about Special Education, nor do they deal with internships in educational institutions that accept them. This is important, because it is difficult to find students with high abilities, hearing impairment or vision impairment in mainstream classrooms. However, autistic children are more common, as well as those with learning difficulties such as dysgraphia, dyslalia, dyscalculia and others.

Now, if the issue of contact with the disabled is a serious one in the context of training, we have to think about the compulsory internship. According to CNE/CP Resolution No. 2/2002, the workload is established as follows: "II - 400 (four hundred) hours of supervised curricular internship from the beginning of the second half of the course according to the document by Brasil (2002) and it is important to complement this with what is contained in the Law of Guidelines and Bases for National Education (LDBN/96) which establishes in its Sole Paragraph of Article 61 the following term: "II - the association between theories and practices, through supervised internships and in-service training". (BRASIL, 1996, p. 46)

In this sense, Deimling's (2013, p. 244) understanding is that:

> [...] it is not the role of the Pedagogy course to train specialists in Special Education. However, we believe it is necessary for these courses to provide future teachers with basic knowledge about these different language codes - or at least a discussion about the existence and importance of each of them in order to prepare them, even minimally, for working with students who have different types of SEN.

When asked **how they felt about their professional qualifications to work with children with disabilities, global developmental disorders and high abilities,** 5 (45%) participants emphatically said no; 4 (35%) reported that they constantly seek qualification; 1 (10%) said that even after graduating and working with this public, they don't feel prepared and 1 (10%) also said that after graduating and specialising, they don't feel prepared. The lack of preparation is present in the following reports:

> No. The person who works with this type of child has to learn a lot and must be highly qualified (P1);
> Not 100 per cent qualified. The first diagnosis is always the teacher's (P2);
> In general, you're never prepared for what you're going to find in the resource room, so this requires more in-depth study, training, the search for knowledge so that we can be, I wouldn't say 100 per cent, because every day there's a different situation (P3);
> Although I work with children in my classroom who have these disorders, disabilities and high abilities, it's a challenge that I've been dealing with for three years and I don't feel prepared (P4);
> I don't think I'm ready today (P5);
> As soon as I finished my post-graduation, I thought I had a little bit, but then I realise every day that I don't know anything. Parents are becoming more and more informed (P6);
> I don't consider myself qualified to work with such an audience (P7);
> Feeling qualified is very challenging. We have to search constantly, because every day the terms change, the proposals change... By seeking out information, I feel more prepared today than I did when I was an undergraduate (P8);
> No. I still have a lot to learn and the school doesn't give me the support to work with this audience (P9);
> Depending on the process the child is going through, depending on the needs they have, perhaps yes... others may not be within our theoretical power. Others may not be within our theoretical power and that's why you should always seek knowledge (P10);
> We try to do a good job, but it's a question of always studying, reading, learning. I'm always looking for qualifications (P11).

It's interesting to note that the lack of preparation is unanimous and evident in the reports. This is extremely serious given the current educational context, although those in the field claim to be in constant search of knowledge, with theory playing a key role in practice.

In this context, it should be added that the demands made on teachers' training and preparation for the act of educating are relevant, but many other aspects must be taken into account when it comes to teaching someone something, especially in the environment known as school.

It's common for teachers to dedicate themselves to their educational work outside of class time, either to gain more knowledge - usually with evening and weekend classes - or to prepare and make teaching and pedagogical resources. In other words, the working hours of education professionals go beyond the time when they are in the classroom and this doesn't seem to be remembered or considered when it comes to demands and requirements so that the results become evident.

What support or means do teachers have for acquiring knowledge and acting in a meaningful way in their work environment, even if they sometimes, and let's say often, have to rely on personal financial resources to carry out their work?

Given the many discussions that have taken place and that permeate education, including special education, it is now possible for these students to have their rights guaranteed, albeit by force of law. However, in order to deal with this public, teachers have had to make efforts that they did not find or prepare them for in their initial training. According to Costa (2015, p. 153)

> The inclusion of students with disabilities requires training that goes beyond the reproduction of pedagogical models, in the sense of enabling the development of student learning through autonomy and through pedagogical experiences that are not yet present in the historical trajectory of teachers, with an emphasis on teachers' attitudes towards inclusive education.

It's important to emphasise that in one of the reports the teacher assures us that the first diagnosis is always the teacher's, but this is a misconception given that the term "diagnosis" is only used for medical professionals. (RELVAS, 2015, p. 52)

It is up to the teacher, by virtue of the law, to accept the impositions of a system that does not allow them to do real work with children who require special attention because they are special.

When asked **what they had to say about the process of qualifying pedagogues to care for children considered to be the target audience of Special Education,** 6 (54%) participants said that the faculty should cover Special Education with more emphasis; 4 (36%) reported that pedagogues should seek knowledge beyond graduation and 1 (10%) believed that a reformulation of academic curricula is already taking place in order to cater for inclusion. The statements below show the configuration of the results:

> The system doesn't help teachers to have this education, this complete training for

> this type of education (P1);
> Nowadays most universities, I believe, have reformulated their curricula a lot because of inclusion, but this inclusion ends up being very theoretical and not very practical (P2);
> This issue has to be worked on a lot because we know that public policies talk a lot about Special Education in theory, but in practice there are no pedagogues prepared to receive this public (P3);
> Pedagogues need to study, not stop studying theory, and develop teaching methods that can facilitate the learning of these children so that inclusion can actually take place (P4);
> I believe that Special Education should be emphasised more. It's given too quickly with superficial concepts (P5);
> As much as we have an area of preference in our degree, Special Education must be targeted and must be well assisted, because the demand has increased and the school is not prepared. The pedagogue who doesn't know what a syndrome is won't be able to stimulate the child (P6);
> The pedagogue's qualification process must be designed to cover all the aspects that enable them to work with this audience, and the pedagogy course doesn't qualify us (P7);
> The first step is to understand what a child with special needs is. Once you've found out, make the right interventions, because we make a lot of mistakes when it comes to interventions. I think it's extremely important for schools to invest in their teachers' qualifications, but much more so for them to allow themselves to seek out new knowledge, study, take courses... try to have contact with other people who deal with this audience (P8);
> I think the university should prepare students better. There should be an internship just for this area, and then we would feel more qualified to work with this public (P9);
> He needs to improve his literature. They need to look for practice to go hand in hand with theory. Professionals who aspire to be pedagogues need to keep studying, keep learning, open their minds to being able to read, to be with this audience and really contribute to the social, psychological and emotional growth of these learners (P10);
> They must seek to qualify, to update themselves, because teachers, educators and pedagogues are eternal researchers!" (P11).

The points of view are genuine, but many of them converge on a single point: that the pedagogue should never stop seeking knowledge in order to be able to do a good job with the target audience of Special Needs Education, and they again point to the same point - training/qualification.

CNE/CP Opinion No. 9/2001 states that inclusion must take place from basic education onwards in order to integrate students with special needs, and continues: "This requires that the training of teachers at the different stages of basic education include knowledge relating to the education of these students". (BRASIL, 2001, p. 26)

However, Deimling (2013) argues that:

> We believe that an important factor that can jeopardise the process of making inclusion a reality in schools is the lack of adequate initial training that provides the future teacher who will work in the regular education system, among other elements, with basic knowledge about the teaching and learning process of students with SEN.

So, as I said at the start of the questioning, continuity of studies and training was emphasised as essential, but it is not possible to see, even in the bibliographies that deal with the subject, anything that confirms or corroborates pedagogical training, which is only something that covers Special Education.

CHAPTER 6

FINAL CONSIDERATIONS

In Early Childhood Education, educating and caring are inseparable actions, since it is the child's responsibility to develop fully and integrally, and the relationship with others and with the environment is a precondition and indispensable for this to happen.

Based on this principle, Early Childhood Education was successfully recognised under the law from the moment its rights as a citizen were recognised, as well as respect for its status as a child and childhood.

As far as special education is concerned, it is possible to find special children socialising with others in regular classrooms, in both public and private schools, albeit from a considerably reduced perspective, and this result is the fruit of arduous struggles, including the prejudice and segregation faced by this public over the decades.

It should be emphasised that even with all the achievements made so far in terms of enrolling and staying in a school, it is still a challenge for special needs children, as barriers still need to be overcome so that they can be effectively cared for under the same learning conditions as others.

Given this reality, the aim of this study was to investigate the perceptions of pedagogues working in early childhood education in relation to their professional qualifications for the care of children considered to be the target audience for special education.

Considering the objectives of the research, it was possible to identify that the content and workload allocated to Special Education subjects, as well as compulsory internships, do not include institutions that have children considered to be the target audience for Special Education. Furthermore, it became clear that the participants' knowledge about the care of children with disabilities, global developmental disorders and high abilities/giftedness is insufficient for them to deal with the learning, specifically, of the children who are part of this group.

In an attempt to work with children with special needs, teachers are constantly seeking relevant and necessary knowledge, either through specialisation or training, as a way of helping these children in their cognitive development process.

In view of the responses obtained regarding the target audience of Special Education, as well as the difficulty observed through the research into the aspects that interfere and/or hinder this child's learning, it became necessary to seek better clarification regarding the terminology used in learning and Special Education, in view of the range of issues that arise every day in the classroom, which are difficult to explain or resolve, based on the principle that learning stems from brain functioning, which is the underlying structure of cognition among all other physical/corporeal functions.

As for the process of including young children with disabilities, global developmental disorders and high abilities, although their educational care is supported by laws, including international organisations, we know that we are falling short of the expectations of effectively implementing inclusion for this public. The reasons for this are structural and methodological problems and, most importantly, adequate training for the education professionals who will be dealing with these children.

In this sense, it is important to clarify that the qualification of the Pedagogue from the perspective of inclusion, although it has undergone many reformulations since its institution, must be revised so that it takes into account Special Education both in terms of workload and subjects, as well as compulsory internships.

Another interesting aspect is the imminent need to consider all the attributions that have long been pertinent to the education professional, in this case and specifically to the Pedagogue, who is the agent that deals with Early Childhood Education. Over the years and since its establishment, Early Childhood Education has been given responsibilities that are not pertinent to it, such as schooling through practices that are the same as those applied in primary education, since this stage should be based on the concept of the child and childhood.

From the results obtained from the interviewees, it was possible to conclude that there are significant doubts about the target audience of Special Education that go beyond learning difficulties, disorders and physical/congenital problems. These aspects go beyond the knowledge that a pedagogue has acquired as an undergraduate, as it is understood that in some cases, in essence and perhaps also in practice, the intervention of specific training such as psychology, that of a psychiatrist and sometimes the intervention of a multidisciplinary team is necessary.

As such, there is an urgent need for the relevant educational bodies to revise the curriculum matrices of the pedagogy course so that the target audience of Special Education receives the education appropriate to their needs, because even if the pedagogue obtains basic and primary notions about Special Education, it is known that there is a range of particularities in the classroom that go beyond the knowledge acquired at the time of academic training.

It is also important to consider compulsory internships as a time to work on relating theory to practice and thus provide better pedagogical training with regard to special needs or those with high abilities.

It is therefore necessary to consider that, due to its specificities, Early Childhood Education is a segment of relevance for the proper formation of an individual, and whether this individual is special or has high abilities, makes the process much more worrying in the sense that public institutions must provide adequate conditions for them to be served with well-structured rooms that have ventilation, lighting, furniture and above all professional support for Early Childhood Education.

Finally, it is hoped that this work can contribute to further reflections on the training of education professionals, in this specific case, the initial and continuing training of pedagogues, in a way that meets the real specific educational needs of children in early childhood education and the initial series, in line with the principles of Inclusive Education.

REFERENCES

ANTUNES, Celso. **Inclusion:** the birth of a new pedagogy. São Paulo: Ciranda Cultural, 2008.

ARANHA, Maria Salete Fábio. **Projeto Escola Viva:** garantindo o acesso e permanência de todos os alunos na escola: necessidades Educacionais especiais dos alunos. Brasília: Ministry of Education, Department of Special Education, 2005. Available at: <http://www.histedbr.fe.unicamp.br/acer_histedbr/seminario/seminario7/TRABALHOS/E/Enio%20rodrigues%20da%20rosa.pdf>. Accessed on: 25 July 2016.

ARANHA, Maria Lúcia de Arruda. **History of Education.** 2. ed. São Paulo: Moderna, 1996.

BALLONE, G. J. What are Mental Disorders. In. **PsiqWeb,** Internet. 2008. Available at: <www.psiqweb.med.br>. Accessed on: 27 Nov. 2016.

BRANDÃO, Carlos Rodrigues. **What is education?** São Paulo: Brasiliense, 2007 (First Steps Collection).

BRAZIL. Constitution (1988). **Constitution of the Federative Republic of Brazil.** Brasília, DF: Senate, 1988.

. Ministry of Education and Sports. Department of Basic Education. **Referencial Curricular Nacional para a Educação Infantil:** Introdução, v.1. Brasília: MEC/SEF, 1998.

. Ministry of Education. Basic Education Secretariat. **National Curriculum Guidelines for** Early Childhood Education/Secretariat of Basic Education. Brasília : MEC, SEB, 2010.Available at: <http://portal.mec.gov.br/index.php?option=com_docman&view=download&alias=97 69-diretrizescurriculares-2012&category_slug=janeiro-2012-pdf&Itemid=30192>. Accessed on: 27 November 2016.

. Ministry of Education. **Base Nacional Comum Curricular.** 2. ver. rev. Brasília:

MEC/SEF, 2016. Available at: <http://basenacionalcomum.mec.gov.br/documentos/bncc-2versao.revista.pdf>. Accessed on: 27 Nov. 2016.

. [Statute of the child and adolescent (1990)]. **Child and adolescent statute and related legislation [electronic resource]:** Law n. 8.069, of 13 July 1990, and related legislation. 12. ed. Brasília: Câmara dos Deputados, Edições Câmara, 2014. (Série legislação; n. 122). Available at: <http://www2.camara.leg.br/responsabilidade-social/acessibilidade/legislacao- pdf/estatuto-da-crica-e-do-adolescente>. Accessed on: 25 March 2016.

. [**LDB nacional [electronic resource]:** Lei de diretrizes e bases da educação nacional: Lei n° 9.394,de 20 de dezembro de 1996, que estabelece as diretrizes e bases da educação nacional. 11. ed. Brasília: Câmara dos Deputados, Edições Câmara, 2015 (Série legislação; n. 159). Available at:<http://www2.camara.leg.br/documentos-e-esquisa/publicacoes/edicoes/paginas-individuais-dos-livros/lei-de-diretrizes-e- bases-da-educacao-nacional>. Accessed on: 25 March 2016.

Ministry of Education and Sport. Department of Basic Education. **Special education from the perspective of inclusive education.** Brasília: MEC/SEF. (Pedagogical Notebooks Series; n. 13). Available at:<http://portal. mec.gov.br/index.php?option=com_docman&view=download&ali as=12334-educacaoespecial-pdf&Itemid=30192>. Accessed on: 25 March 2016.

. Knowledge and practices of inclusion: recommendations for building inclusive schools. 2. ed. General coordination SEESP/MEC. Brasília: MEC, Secretariat of Special Education, 2006 (Series: Knowledge and practices of inclusion). Available at:<http://portal.mec.gov.br/seesp/arquivos/pdf/cadernocoordenador.pdf.>. Accessed on: 25 March 2016.

. Law n. 13.146. Brasília, DF: Subchefia para Assuntos Jurídicos, 2015. Available at: <http://www.planalto.gov.br/ccivil_03/_Ato2015- 2018/2015/Lei/L13146.htm>. Accessed on: 25 March 2016.

. Decree No. 3.298, of 20 December 1999. Regulates Law No. 7.853, of 24 October 1989, provides for the National Policy for the Integration of People with Disabilities, consolidates protection rules, and makes other provisions. **Official Gazette of the Federative Republic of Brazil,** Executive Branch, Brasília, DF, 21 December 1999. Section 1. Available at: <http://www.planalto.gov.br/ccivil_03/decreto/D3298.htm#art60>. Accessed on: 10 September 2016.

. Law No. 010172, of 9 January 2001. Approves the National Education Plan and makes other provisions. Brasília, DF: Sub-Cabinet for Legal Affairs, 2001. Available at: <http://portal.mec.gov.br/arquivos/pdf/L10172.pdf>. Accessed on: 18 September 2016.

. CNE/CP Opinion No. 9, 2001. Provides for the National Curriculum Guidelines for the Training of Basic Education Teachers, at higher education level, full degree course. **Official Gazette of the Federative Republic** of **Brazil,** Executive Branch, Brasília, DF, 18 January 2001. Section 1, p. 31. Available at: <http://portal.mec.gov.br/cne/arquivos/pdf/009.pdf>. Accessed on: 18 September 2016.

. Ordinance No. 948. **National Policy for Special Education from the Perspective of Inclusive Education.** Brasília, DF: MEC/SECADI, 2007. Available at: <http://portal.mec.gov.br/index.php?option=com_docman&view=download&alias= 16690-

politica-nacional-de-educacao-especial-na-perspectiva-da-educacao- inclusiva-05122014&Itemid=30192>. Accessed on: 18 September 2016.

. **Distance Continuing Education for Teachers of Specialised Educational Assistance:** mental disability. SEESP/SEED. Brasília: MEC, Secretariat for Special Education, 2007. Available at: <http://portal.mec.gov.br/seesp/arquivos/pdf/aee_dm.pdf> Accessed on: 13 Nov. 2016.

. **Distance Continuing Education for Teachers of Specialised Educational Assistance:** visual impairment. SEESP/SEED. Brasília: MEC, Secretariat for Special Education, 2007. Available at: <http://portal.mec.gov.br/seesp/arquivos/pdf/aee_dv.pdf> Accessed on: 13 Nov. 2016

. **Continued Distance Training for Teachers of Specialised Educational Assistance:** people with deafblindness. SEESP/SEED. Brasília: MEC, Secretariat for Special Education, 2007. Available at: <http://portal.mec.gov.br/seesp/arquivos/pdf/aee_da - surdez.pdf> Accessed on: 13 Nov. 2016

. Resolution No. 4, of 2 October 2009. Establishes Operational Guidelines for Specialised Educational Assistance in Basic Education, Special Education modality. Federal Official Gazette, Brasília, DF, 24 September 2009. In: BRAZIL, Ministry of Education. Secretariat for Basic Education. Secretariat for Continuing Education, Literacy, Diversity and Inclusion. Secretariat for Professional and Technological Education. National Education Council. National Chamber of Basic Education. **General National Curriculum Guidelines for Basic Education.** Ministry of Education. Department of Basic Education. Directorate of Curricula and Integral Education. Brasília: MEC, SEB, DICEI, 2013.

BIAGGIO, Rita de. The inclusion of children with disabilities grows and changes the practice of nurseries and pre-schools. **Child magazine.** Ministério da Educação, n. 44, nov. 2007, p. 19-26. Available at: <http://portal.mec.gov.br/seb/arquivos/pdf/Educinf/revista44.pdf>. Accessed on: 26 March 2016.

CANCINO, Miguel Higuera. **Developmental and communication disorders:** autism - strategies and practical solutions. 2. ed. Rio de Janeiro: WAK Editora, 2015.

CARVALHO, Rosita Edler. Integration and inclusion: what are we talking about? In: **Salto para o Futuro:** Educação Especial: tendências atuais / Secretaria de Educação a Distância. Brasília: Ministry of Education, SEED, 1999 (Series of Studies. Distance Education, v.9). Available at: <http://www.dominiopublico.gov.br/download/texto/me002692.pdf>. Accessed on: 04 Dec. 2016.

CERISARA, Ana Beatriz. The National Curriculum Framework for Early Childhood Education in the context of reforms. **Revista Educação e Sociedade.** Campinas, v. 23, n. 80, September/2002, p. 326-345. Available at: <http://www.scielo.br/pdf/es/v23n80/12935.pdf>. Accessed on: 08 Feb. 2016.

CHAHINI, Thelma Helena Costa. **Social attitudes and opinions of teachers and students at the federal university of maranhão in relation to the inclusion of students with disabilities in higher education.** Thesis presented to the Postgraduate Programme in Education, Faculty of Philosophy and Sciences, Paulista State University - UNESP - Marília Campus, 2010. Available at: <https://www.marilia.unesp.br/Home/Pos-

Graduacao/Educacao/Dissertacoes/chahini_thc_do_mar.pdf>. Accessed on: 10 July 2016.

CINTRA, Flávia. In: **The Convention on the Rights of Persons with Disabilities, Commented** (Coord.) Ana Paula Crosara Resende and Flávia Maria de Paiva Vital. Brasília: Special Secretariat for Human Rights. National Coordination for the Integration of People with Disabilities, 2008.

COSENZA, Ramon M.; GUERRA, Leonor B. **Neuroscience and Education:** how the brain learns. Porto Alegre: Artmed, 2011.

COSTA, Valdelúcia Alves da. The demands of inclusive teacher training and practice under the aegis of human rights. In: (eds) SILVA, Aida Maria Monteiro; COSTA, Valdelúcia Alves da. **Inclusive education and human rights:** contemporary perspectives. São Paulo: Cortez, 2015 (Human rights education collection).

COSTA, Ursula Thomé. Sensory disabilities: sight and hearing. In: BRITO, Adrian Rocha (et. al); MAIA, Heber (org.). **Special educational needs.** Rio de Janeiro: Wak Editora, 2011 (Neuroeducação, vol. 3).

CRAVEIRO, Clélia Brandão Alvarenga. Report on CNE/CEB Opinion No. 13/2009. In: BRAZIL, Ministry of Education. Secretariat for Basic Education. Secretariat for Continuing Education, Literacy, Diversity and Inclusion. Secretariat for Professional and Technological Education. National Education Council. National Chamber of Basic Education. **General National Curriculum Guidelines for Basic Education.** Ministry of Education. Department of Basic Education. Directorate of Curricula and Integral Education. Brasília: MEC, SEB, DICEI, 2013.

CRUZ, Gisele Barreto da. **Pedagogy course in Brazil:** history and training with primordial pedagogues. Rio de Janeiro: Wak Editora, 2011.

SALAMANCA DECLARATION. On Principles, Policies and Practices in the Field of Special Needs Education. Needs. Available at: <http://portal.mec.gov.br/seesp/arquivos/pdf/salamanca.pdf>. Accessed on: 22 July 2016.

DEFICIENTESONLINE. Available at: <http://www.deficienteonline.com.br/deficiencia-fisica-tipos-e-definicoes12.html.>
Accessed on: 13 Nov. 2016.

DEIMLING, Natalia Neves Macedo. Special Education in Pedagogy courses: considerations on teacher training for school inclusion. **Revista Educação Unisinos.** v. 17, n. 3, Sep/Dec 2013. Available at: <http://revistas.unisinos.br/index.php/educacao/article/viewFile/edu.2013.173.08/381 5>. Accessed on 11 September 2016.

DELOU, Cristina Maria Carvalho. High Abilities. In: BRITO, Adrian Rocha (et. al); MAIA, Heber (org.). **Necessidades Educacionais especiais.** Rio de Janeiro: Wak Editora, 2011 (Neuroeducação, vol. 3).

DIFFERENT DISABILITIES AND THEIR CONCEPTS. Available at: <http://www.mpgo.mp.br/portalweb/hp/41/docs/diferentes_deficiencias_e_seus_conc eitos.pdf>. Accessed on: 13 Nov. 2016.

FERREIRA, Aurélio Buarque de Holanda. **Novo Dicionário Eletrónico Aurélio version**

7.0. 5. ed. do Dicionário Aurélio da Língua Portuguesa Positivo Informática. 2010. Not paginated.

FREITAS, S. N. Teacher training in inclusive education: building the basis of the whole process. In: RODRIGUES, D. (Org.). **Inclusão e educação:** doze olhares sobre a inclusão inclusiva. São Paulo: Summus, 2006. p. 161-181.

GARCIA, Rosalba Maria Cardoso. Special education policy from an inclusive perspective and teacher training in Brazil. **Revista Brasileira de Educação,** v. 18 n. 52, jan.-mar. 2013, p. 101-239.Available at: <http://www.scielo.br/pdf/rbedu/v18n52/07.pdf>. Accessed on: 26 March 2016.

GIL, Antônio Carlos. **Methods and techniques of social research.** 6. ed. 6. reimp. São Paulo: Atlas, 2014.

GODOFFREDO, Vera Lúcia Flor Sénéchal de. How to train teachers for an inclusive school? In: **Salto para o Futuro:** Educação Especial: tendências atuais / Secretaria de Educação a Distância. Brasília: Ministry of Education, SEED, 1999 (Series of Studies. Distance Education, v.9). Available at: <http://www.dominiopublico.gov.br/download/texto/me002692.pdf>. Accessed on: 04 Dec. 2016.

GOMES, Vanessa Fonseca; BOSA, Cleonice. Stress and family relationships from the perspective of siblings of individuals with global developmental disorders. **Estud. psicol.** (Natal), Natal, v. 9, n. 3, p. 553-561, dez. 2004 . Available at: <http://www.scielo.br/scielo.php?script=sci_arttext&pid=S1413-294X2004000300018&lng=en&nrm=iso>. Accessed on: 10 September 2016.

GÓMEZ, Ana María Salgado. TERÁN, Nora Espinosa. **Learning difficulties:** detection and help strategies. 2. ed. Cultural: São Paulo, 2009.

LIBÂNEO, José Carlos; OLIVEIRA, João Ferreira de; TOSCHI, Mirza Seabra. **School education:** policies, structure and organisation. 10. ed. rev. and expanded. São Paulo: Cortez, 2012 (Coleção docência em formação: saberes pedagógicos).

LIBÂNEO, José Carlos. **Pedagogy and pedagogues, for what?** 12. ed. São Paulo: Cortez, 2010.

MAIA, Heber. Cerebral Palsy. In: BRITO, Adrian Rocha (et. al); MAIA, Heber (org.). **Necessidades Educacionais especiais.** Rio de Janeiro: Wak Editora, 2011 (Neuroeducação, vol. 3).

MAZZOTA, Marcos José Silveira. **Special Education in Brazil:** History and Public Policies. 5. ed. São Paulo: Cortez, 2005.

RELVAS, Marta Pires. **Neurosciences and learning disorders:** multiple efficiencies for inclusive education. 6. ed. Rio de Janeiro: Wak Editora, 2015.

ROSA, Enio Rodrigues da; DUTRA, Martinha Clarete. **Blind people:** work, history, education and organisation in Brazil. Londrina - Paraná (Dissertation) Master's in Education, UNICAMP. Available at: <http://www.histedbr.fe.unicamp.br/acer_histedbr/seminario/seminario7/TRABALHOS/E/Enio%20rodrigues%20da%20rosa.pdf>. Accessed on: 25 July 2016.

SANCHES, Emília Cipriano. **Creche:** reality and ambiguities. 2. ed. Petrópolis, Rio de Janeiro: Vozes, 2003.

SILVA, Aida Maria Monteiro. Teacher training from the perspective of inclusive education and the link with human rights. In: (eds) SILVA, Aida Maria Monteiro; COSTA, Valdelúcia Alves da. **Inclusive education and human rights:** contemporary perspectives. São Paulo: Cortez, 2015 (Human rights education collection).

TENGAN, Sérgio K.; MAIA, Anne K. Functional psychoses in childhood and adolescence.**Jornal de Pediatria,** vol. 80, n. 2(supl), 2004. Available at: <http://www.scielo.br/pdf/jped/v80n2s0/v80n2Sa02.pdf>. Accessed on: 13 Nov. 2016.

MIX
Papier aus verantwortungsvollen Quellen
Paper from responsible sources
FSC® C105338

Printed by Books on Demand GmbH, Norderstedt / Germany